FAITH IN THE FIRE

LEEANN DEON

For permission requests, email the publisher:

Attention: Permissions Coordinator

Welcome To The Storm Publishing!

Granbury, Texas

info@w2tspublishing.org

https://w2tspublishing.org/

Ordering Information:

Quantity sales. Special discounts are available on quantity purchases by corporations, associations, and others. For details, contact the publisher at the email address above.

Library of Congress Control Number: 2025906248

Orders by U.S. trade bookstores and wholesalers.

ISBN: 978-1-966612-17-9

Cover Design: Asghar Saim

Editing by Ambrose Edit

First Printed Edition: May 2025

Printed in the United States of America

Table of Contents

PROLOGUE

A Stormy Beginning

Storms shape us in ways we never anticipate. Some strike without warning, tearing through our lives and leaving behind wreckage and unanswered questions. Others gather slowly, cloud by cloud, until we find ourselves in the midst of a tempest we never saw coming.

My life began in a storm, a place of pain, uncertainty, and struggle. But within that storm, I discovered something far greater than hardship. I found resilience. I found redemption. And above all, I found the undeniable power of faith.

There was a time when I doubted my ability to make it through. The weight of my past, the wounds of my struggles, and the voices of doubt tried to convince me that I was too broken to be made whole. But God had a different plan.

He took what was shattered and made it beautiful.

He led me from darkness to light, from despair to purpose.

Today, I stand as a teacher, a mentor, and a leader, pouring into the lives of others, especially those who, like me, have faced hardships that once threatened to define them. I work with students the world often overlooks, guiding them with patience and love. I walk alongside women and youth in my church, sharing the same hope that once saved me.

My life is a testament to what God can do when we trust Him, even when we cannot see the way forward.

This book is my journey

A story of storms and survival.

Of breaking and becoming.

Of faith that refuses to waver.

It is for anyone who has ever felt lost.

Anyone who has wondered if healing is possible.

Anyone who needs a reminder that no storm lasts forever.

No matter how fierce the winds may blow, there is always hope.

And if you're willing to hold on, you just might find that the very storm meant to break you is the one that sets you free

CHAPTER 1

The Foundation of Strength

My childhood shadows shaped my strength long before I took my first breath. Challenges emerged early, like when Satan tried to convince my mother I was a tumor, but I came into this world resilient. Born at 8 lbs. 4 oz. after 19 grueling hours of labor, I arrived on Mother's Day, a yearly reminder of my mother's sacrifices, as she missed out on candy and flowers. To this day, we still laugh about it.

My journey began in Kansas City, Missouri, where the seeds of survival were planted early. At just two years old, a scalding accident during one of my father's beloved hot baths altered the course of my life. That incident prompted my family to relocate to Oklahoma, a turning point that surrounded me with love and care.

Growing up with two older siblings, I found my first best friend in my sister, who was only 11 months older. My brother, a few years my senior, was the family's shining star, his brilliance extending beyond the basketball court. I often think back to a night spent wandering through the rain to my great-grandmother's house, where her gentle spirit wrapped around me like a warm blanket. My father watched over us while my mother and grandmother worked overnight, yet fear was a stranger to me. Later, life gifted me with a baby sister, further enriching our family's dynamic.

However, as my parents faced their struggles and eventually divorced, each hardship became a building block for the person I would become. My mother, who had me at just 20, endured countless difficulties but possessed a strength that inspired me profoundly. I wanted to be just like her as I navigated my childhood.

My father, on the other hand, was largely absent. He left when I was young, and our relationship was almost nonexistent, I can barely recall him visiting more than a couple of times. One memory stands out vividly. At my uncle's funeral in Kansas City, a cousin approached him and asked if he knew me. He studied me for a moment before replying, "She looks familiar." My heart shattered. He didn't even recognize me. Moments later, he walked away without offering so much as a hug.

On another occasion, I visited his home, only to be told I couldn't speak to my half-sister. At that moment, it felt like a final goodbye. The pain was profound. When he passed away, it was heartbreaking to refrain from attending his funeral, especially knowing that his wife had chosen not to include us in the obituary.

Despite this, my grandmother, who lived across the street from us along with my aunts and uncles, never wavered in their love and support. They filled our lives with warmth and stability. I often struggled to understand how a father could walk away from his children, and the pain of that abandonment lingered for years. However, being raised in a holiness church and living with my maternal grandmother instilled in me the values of forgiveness and compassion. I knew I didn't want to harbor hatred toward my father. Instead, I found myself making excuses for his absence, clinging to the belief that there was a divine plan at work.

In the third grade, we were blessed with a wonderful stepfather whose acceptance and love transformed our lives. I am deeply grateful for his kindness. My mother, a talented beautician, opened a shop in our home, while my stepfather, Willie Earl Hersey, dedicated himself to his job at the Union Pacific Railroad. Life with him was filled with adventure. He loved golfing, and our family frequently traveled between Arkansas and Kansas City to visit relatives.

He was an extraordinary man, full of humor, wisdom, and an infectious zest for life. He took immense pride in his shiny Cadillac and his Stacy Adams shoes, and I still remember how much he loved to dance.

During my school years, my father would occasionally tell my mother how smart I was, even though my grades didn't always reflect it. I was simply too caught up in the whirlwind of life to focus on academics. But my mother always stood by me, reminding him that not everyone excels in the same way. Years later, after my father had passed, I earned straight A's in college. My mother lovingly reminded me that she had always believed in me, and that acknowledgment made me feel incredibly special.

There was a moment when I deeply wished I could share my success with my father, to show him what I was capable of and make him proud. But deep down, I knew he would have been proud of me regardless. God has a way of removing certain people from our lives while bringing others in to uplift and shape us. I am forever grateful for my stepfather's unwavering support, especially in sports, as he patiently taught me how to play golf.

He was the first African-American member of the golf course in Nowata, Oklahoma. Together, he and my mother provided us with a life where we never lacked for much. Their combined strength and dedication shaped my life in ways I will always cherish.

I often reflect on the generational trauma and behaviors that were passed down, rejection, fear, anger, rebellion, abandonment, and low self-esteem. But in that same breath, I also see the resilience, strength, and survival that emerged from it.

My older brother lived with my grandmother just a street away, but in our little country town, we were inseparable. He played basketball and later went on to college, though I believe our father's absence deeply impacted him. As a young man, it must have been painful to embark on new endeavors without our dad to share in those moments. My brother is a handsome and talented athlete who even played overseas. Intelligent, well-rounded, and a great communicator, he continues to be a source of inspiration in my life.

My oldest sister and I are just eleven months apart in age, and in many ways, she has always felt more like a second mother than just a sibling. Growing up, she was my constant companion, sharing a room with me, teaching me everything from how to tie my shoes to the joy of singing. According to her, I was her true best friend.

She has always been one of my biggest cheerleaders, ready to support me and my children in any way possible. I have vivid memories of our childhood antics, like the time she attempted to make homemade potato chips. What started as an exciting experiment quickly turned disastrous when smoke billowed from the kitchen, leaving thick, dark stains on the ceiling. In a panic, she dashed out of the house, and we both scrambled to clean up the mess before our parents returned home.

Despite the chaos, her intelligence always shone through. She had a gift for problem-solving, whether it was fixing childhood mishaps or navigating the complexities of adulthood. We have always been exceptionally close, and she remains a source of wisdom and strength in my life. The bond we formed as children is just as strong today.

My younger sister has shown incredible strength, giving my mother a run for her money. She always found her own path, pursuing her desires with determination. From a life filled with drinking and partying, she transformed herself, quitting cold turkey after many years. She became a chef, the best cook I know, and above all, a loving wife, mother, and grandmother. Seeing God's hand in her life, I know she is truly my MVP.

Looking back, I see how generational trauma was passed down, rejection, fear, anger, rebellion, abandonment, and low self-esteem. But in that same reflection, I also see resilience, strength, and survival. I have learned that while we inherit the pain of our ancestors, we also inherit their strength to overcome.

CHAPTER 2

Breaking the Chains of the Past

Growing up, I never fully realized how deeply my past shaped my identity. The experiences of my childhood seeped into my adulthood in ways I couldn't yet comprehend. I carried the wounds of my father's absence, the weight of my mother's struggles, and the silent battles I fought within myself.

Rebellion became my refuge from pain. I resisted structure, defied authority, and clung to independence, convinced that relying on others would only lead to disappointment. I found myself trapped in cycles passed down through generations, cycles of distrust, broken relationships, and pushing people away before they had the chance to leave.

Yet, through it all, God was at work within me, slowly breaking the chains that bound me to my past.

The Weight of Generational Trauma

Generational trauma runs deep. It weaves through families, shaping behaviors and beliefs in ways we often don't recognize until we're old enough to step back and see the patterns. For me, some of those patterns were glaring, drinking, cursing, staying in relationships too long, and shutting down emotionally instead of facing my feelings. At the time, I didn't realize I was merely mirroring what I had seen growing up.

Drinking felt natural because it was a part of my environment. It wasn't questioned; it was normalized. Cursing came just as easily, I spoke like a sailor, a habit I'm still working on. But praise God, I've made progress. I remember the day my mother looked at me and asked, "Do you praise God with the same mouth you curse with?" That question hit me like a slap in the face. It forced me to pause and reflect. I had to repent. From that moment, I made a conscious effort to change, to be mindful of the words I spoke. Not every word that left my mouth was a curse anymore.

Holding on to relationships longer than I should have, that was another pattern I inherited. I grew up watching my parents stay in situations that weren't healthy for them, so I learned to do the same. I clung to relationships, hoping things would change, believing love alone could mend what was broken. But that cycle only led to heartache and exhaustion. It took me years to understand that love isn't about how much pain you can endure. Real love means knowing when to walk away.

Then there was the pain of abandonment. My father was absent, and his absence left wounds that bled into every part of my life, abandonment issues, low self-esteem, emotional walls, and a pattern of shutting down rather than opening up. I carried all of it. But even in my brokenness, I refused to let those wounds define me. My biological father may have struggled in some areas, but I chose strength. I made up my mind: the patterns of my past would not become the inheritance of the next generation.

The Strength of My Mother

If I had to name the generational curses I carried, the list would be long, adultery, drinking, cursing, anger, jealousy, envy, and strife. A hardened heart. Being molested added another layer of trauma, and feeling abandoned by my father only deepened the wounds. I had to confront all of these struggles head-on, and it wasn't easy.

But one thing I know for certain, prayer changed everything. My loved ones prayed for me, and I prayed for myself. I longed for something better. I knew, without a doubt, that God was always with me. Because of that, I refused to remain bound by what had been passed down. I had the power to break the cycle.

Through it all, my mother remained my rock.

CHAPTER 3

The Path to Redemption

I found myself standing at the crossroads between who I was and who I aspired to become. In my darkest moments, God's call echoed the loudest. The journey was far from easy, but with each step toward healing, I uncovered a new version of myself, one no longer defined by past wounds but by the strength to rise above them.

As a teenager, I grappled with the weight of generational trauma. It shaped my actions, influenced my relationships, and guided my decisions. I wrestled with anger, felt the deep sting of my father's absence, and often made choices driven by pain rather than purpose. Yet, even when I failed to see it, God's hand was always upon me.

The Struggles of My Teenage Years

By the time I was 13, I had already tasted alcohol. My stepdad kept bottles of Mad Dog 20/20 in the refrigerator, deep purple, sweet, and strong. It was dangerously easy to drink. My friends and I would sneak sips whenever no one was watching. That was the beginning of a reckless spiral.

Looking back, my behavior was completely out of control. I smoked cigarettes, not just occasionally, but regularly. I remember the day I got caught with a whole pack hidden under my bed. My stepdad found them, and instead of punishing me, he just said, "Give them to me." He was a smoker too.

I fought all the time. I skipped school whenever I felt like it. My grades were a disaster, D's and F's filled my report cards like stains I couldn't scrub off. I had no motivation to do better. Teachers were just obstacles, rules were suggestions, and I lived by my own terms. I cursed out teachers, got in trouble constantly, and didn't care. School felt like a prison sentence I had no intention of serving.

The only thing that kept me somewhat connected to reality was basketball. I loved sports. I loved moving, competing, and pushing myself. But the moment I sat in a classroom, listening to teachers drone on about things that felt meaningless, I checked out completely. I wanted no part of it.

My stepdad would shake his head at my grades and say, "D's? She should be doing better than that." My mother, though, always defended me. "Everybody doesn't learn the same way," she'd argue. She meant well, but to me, it felt like permission to keep doing whatever I wanted.

When I got in trouble at school, they called home, but I had already figured out ways to avoid consequences. Detention? I didn't care. A paddling? Nobody was going to lay a hand on me. If things got too bad, I'd just walk out. Sometimes, I'd go home on foot. Other times, I'd call my mom to come pick me up. Nobody could really control me, I was running my own life, even if I was running it straight into chaos.

A Reckless Path

I had a reputation as the class clown. I wouldn't call myself a bully, but I made sure no one got bullied around me. If I saw someone being picked on, I stepped in. But the sad part? No one ever asked what was really going on with me.

No one wondered why I was so angry. Why I acted out. Why I didn't care about school. People just accepted it. That's just how she is.

But I was hurting. And nobody noticed.

To escape, I started hanging out with older kids. I spent hours at the arcade, crashed at random houses, and drank. I had no real sense of danger. I barely knew these people, but I trusted them anyway. Now, as an adult, I see how reckless that was. I could have been taken advantage of, hurt, or worse.

I was a young Black girl running with white kids, disappearing for hours, and no one even knew where I was. But even as I was making my bed in hell, God was covering me.

The Wake-Up Call

Eventually, my reckless behavior caught up with me. In eighth grade, I was expelled from my middle school. Kicked out. They sent me to an all-white, rural school, a completely different world.

Around that time, I lost a close friend to an overdose. Not long after, another friend fell ill and passed away. Death hit me in a way I wasn't prepared for. It forced me to see that life wasn't just one big joke. It wasn't just about skipping school and hanging out. People were dying. And for the first time, I started to wonder, was I next?

Even then, I still felt lost. People don't realize what kids go through when no one talks to them, when they're just expected to survive. I was at a point where I didn't care about anything. I had been spoiled, shielded from real consequences.

I felt untouchable. I was going to do what I wanted, who was going to stop me?

But something was shifting. I didn't know it yet, but the seeds of change had already been planted. And soon, I would be forced to face everything I had been running from.

A Life-Altering Moment

Some moments in life change you forever. They shape how you see yourself, how you trust others, and the choices you make. I was 15 when my world shifted.

My sister and I often visited Coffeyville, Kansas to spend time with our grandmother. She had cancer and had moved to Kansas for treatment, so we traveled back and forth to see her, spend time together, and get away for a while.

One night, we needed a ride to Coffeyville. My uncle usually took us, but this time, another guy we knew offered to drive. I didn't think much of it.

For some reason, my sister ended up getting dropped off at home to get ready while I stayed in the car, planning to hang out on the next block until she was done. But instead of taking me where I was supposed to go, he drove somewhere else.

We pulled up near a house, a familiar one, a family member's home, but we weren't stopping for a visit. I was in the backseat when I quickly realized something was wrong. The car door wouldn't open from the inside. The lock was broken.

A wave of panic hit me. I felt trapped, powerless, unsure of what to do. The moment was overwhelming, and I was completely alone.

What happened next is something I never asked for. Something I never consented to. I was taken advantage of in that car—held in place not just by the broken lock, but by fear, confusion, and the awful knowledge that no one was coming to help me. My voice, my body, my choice—it was all disregarded. It didn't matter what I wanted. It didn't matter that I said nothing, or that I couldn't move. My silence wasn't permission. My stillness wasn't a yes.

Afterward, we went back to pick up my sister. I stayed silent.

Because how do you explain a moment that steals so much from you in so little time? How do you speak when your voice feels like it's been buried beneath shame, disbelief, and hurt?

I didn't know what to say. I didn't know who would believe me. So, I said nothing. But that doesn't mean it didn't happen. And it doesn't mean I wasn't forever changed by it.

We made it to Kansas, where my uncle ended up driving us the rest of the way. That night, I sat in my grandmother's house, numb, trying to push everything down. I didn't know how to process what had just happened. I didn't tell a soul.

The Secret I Couldn't Keep

I stayed silent until I had no choice. Months passed before I even realized I was three months pregnant.

My mother and grandmother took me to the doctor. When the test came back positive, I had to speak the truth I had been burying inside. Shame. Fear. Confusion. It all crashed over me at once. They confronted him. He denied everything. He tried to shift the blame. But I knew the truth.

After my baby was born, the shame didn't disappear, it grew heavier. I blamed myself, convinced that somehow, it was my fault. The weight of it suffocated me.

And yet, through all my pain, I clung to my mother. I didn't want her out of my sight. Maybe she didn't understand why. Maybe she wondered why I suddenly needed to be close. But I couldn't help it, she was my safety.

I still remember my grandmother's words when I was pregnant:

"If you have this baby, it will always be taken care of."

She named her.

Six months later, I gave birth to my baby girl. Despite everything, she was never a burden, she was my blessing. Even now, I am proud of her and endlessly grateful. She changed me. She gave me purpose.

I had to learn to forgive, not for him, but for me. I knew that God could deal with people far better than I ever could. Holding onto anger and bitterness would only weigh me down, so I chose to let go. I chose to heal.

CHAPTER 4

Broken, But Not Defeated

After some time, I made a decision for myself, I left for Job Corps in Utah.

It was the longest I had ever been away from my mother, six to eight months. But in that time, I learned how to type, how to live independently, and how to survive without the comfort of home. It was terrifying, yet necessary.

When I returned, I got my own place and took care of my child. I was determined to be a good mother.

Looking back, I reflect on everything I endured, being molested at seven or eight, the trauma I faced at fifteen, becoming a mother at sixteen.

But more than anything, I think about how God covered me. How He transformed my pain into something greater.

I am not a victim. I am a survivor. And though the road was difficult, I wouldn't change a thing. Every step, every struggle, led me here. Stronger. Wiser. Unbreakable.

From Pain to Purpose

Looking back, I think about everything I endured, being molested at 7 or 8, going through what I did at 15, and becoming a mother at 16.

I remember how lost I felt. How broken. How ashamed. But I also remember how God covered me. How He turned my pain into something greater. My daughter saved me in ways she will never understand. She gave me a reason to fight, to push forward, to heal.

I am not a victim. I am a survivor. And though the road was hard, I wouldn't change anything because every step led me here. Stronger. Wiser. Unbreakable.

Walking in Purpose

As I embraced my newfound faith, I realized my pain had prepared me for a greater purpose. I began working with youth who had faced struggles similar to mine, guiding them toward healing and hope. Teaching became more than a job, it became my ministry.

With every student I taught and every conversation I had, I saw reflections of my younger self, searching, hurting, longing for guidance. And in those moments, I knew God had placed me here for a reason. My life, once defined by storms, had become a beacon of hope for others navigating their own darkness it.

Finding Peace in My Purpose

Looking back, I see that every storm, every trial, and every painful chapter of my life was leading me to this moment.

The girl who once felt lost and broken now stands in her purpose, using her story to light the way for others.

My journey is far from over. There are still challenges to face, lessons to learn, and lives to touch. But one thing I know for certain, I am exactly where I'm meant to be.

Teaching, mentoring, serving, this isn't just what I do; it's who I am. And every day, I thank God for guiding me here.

CHAPTER 5

A Mother's Grief and God's Grace

Losing a child is a pain that words can never fully capture. It shatters you in ways you never imagined. It changes you forever.

Years after my daughter was born, I was living in Kansas, caught in a difficult, unhealthy relationship. But despite everything, I held my own. And on August 25, I gave birth to a beautiful baby boy.

He was perfect, six pounds of pure joy. A happy, peaceful baby. He didn't cry much, and his little spirit was gentle. I loved him beyond words.

The Night Everything Changed

I remember that night so clearly. It was early morning when I heard him stir, not crying, just making small sounds, as if he were waking up. I was exhausted. I told his father to check on him, then drifted back to sleep. I guess he did too.

When I woke up that morning, something felt off. A heaviness I couldn't explain. I got up to check on my baby. But my sweet boy was gone. He had passed away in his sleep, just days before Christmas.

The ambulance came, but it was too late. They called it crib death. SIDS. No explanation. No warning. Just… gone.

The Weight of Grief

I felt numb. Lost. Angry. I kept asking, *"Why, God? Why would You let this happen?"*

My mother and stepfather were in Kansas at the time, but even with their presence, I had never felt so alone. The weight of the loss crushed me. I blamed myself. I was his mother, how could I not have known something was wrong? I blamed his father, too. *Why didn't he wake up and check on him? Why didn't I?*

Our relationship couldn't survive the grief. We split up. I don't even remember if we were still together by the time of the funeral. Everything became a blur. I had already lost my grandmother to breast cancer, and now my son. It was too much.

Drowning in the Pain

Drinking became my escape. It dulled the pain, numbed the reality I refused to face. But no matter how much I drank, the pain never truly left.

By this time, my daughter was five years old. She had lost her baby brother, too. She loved holding him, rocking him, caring for him in her own little way. But deep down, I knew I hadn't been there for her the way I should have. I was drowning in my own grief.

I wasn't just mourning my son, I was mourning the future I would never have with him. The first steps, the first words, the birthday parties, the hugs, the laughter. All of it was stolen from me. A parent should never have to bury their child. It goes against everything we believe life should be.

For a long time, I didn't know how to move forward. I didn't know how to breathe, how to function.

But now, looking back, I realize something, God was still there. Even in my pain. Even in my brokenness. Even when I was angry at Him, He never left me.

I've come to understand that the suffering we endure is often preparation. We don't always see God's plan. We don't always understand His will. But through it all, He can still use us.

Losing my son shaped me in ways I never expected. It gave me a heart for others who are grieving. It made me understand pain on a level I never had before.

And because of that, I can say with full sincerity:

"I know what you're going through."

I know the emptiness. I know the hurt. I know the questions that never seem to have answers. I know the weight of a grief that never truly leaves. And I know that even in the darkest, most unbearable moments, God is still working.

Beauty from Ashes

Nothing will ever take away the pain of losing my son. I will always miss him. I will always wonder who he would have been, what he would have become. But I also know that his short life had meaning. His presence, no matter how brief, was not in vain.

There are days when the grief hits me like a wave, sudden and unrelenting, catching me off guard. A scent, a lullaby, a photo tucked away in a drawer—these small moments can bring me to my knees. And yet, even in those moments of sorrow, I feel a quiet strength growing inside me. Not because the pain is gone, but because I've learned to carry it differently.

Some may struggle to understand how you can mourn someone you barely got to know. But a mother knows. From the moment I knew he existed, I loved him with every part of me. I dreamed of his first steps, his first words, his laughter filling our home. I imagined birthday cakes, scraped knees, and school plays. I dreamed of the man he might become—kind, brave, wise beyond his years. And even though those dreams now live only in my heart, they are still real. He is still real.

I've come to see that my son's life, though short, has shaped mine in ways I never expected. He has taught me about resilience, about the depths of love, and about the power of remembrance. His life has fueled a new purpose in me—to honor his memory by living fully, by embracing each moment, and by finding beauty even in the ashes.

There's a kind of sacredness in loss. A clarity. You learn what matters and what doesn't. You see people differently. You love harder, hold tighter, and speak more kindly. My son gave me that gift. A perspective born from pain, but rich with meaning.

CHAPTER 6

A Journey Through Trials, Faith, and Transformation

In the years following my third marriage, life tested my resilience, my faith, and my very existence in ways I never imagined. I had already endured loss, heartbreak, and trauma, yet the trials ahead would become some of the most defining moments of my journey. By all odds, I should have died at least three times.

But God said, "Not so."

The Frist Wake-Up Call - A Head-On Collision

The first accident happened when I reached for my cell phone while driving at night in the rain. I collided head-on with a telephone pole.

The impact shattered me, fracturing my femur, leaving deep facial lacerations, and confining me to a hospital for a month. When I was finally released, I couldn't even sleep in a real bed. Instead, I had to recover in a hospital bed set up in my home.

Each of these accidents could have been the end of my story. But they weren't. Because God wasn't done with me yet.

The Second Close Call - A Plunge into Darkness

Some time later, another accident. This time, it was raining. Dark roads. Wet pavement. A single moment of miscalculation. I drove straight off a 60-foot cliff.

The instant my tires left the ground, time slowed. I was airborne.

In that moment, I cried out to God. I didn't pray for myself, I prayed for my family. *"God, please take care of my children. Please let my mother be okay."*

I braced for impact. The car rolled, over and over. When it finally came to a stop, I was still alive.

I looked down and saw my foot, nearly destroyed. The doctors said I was lucky to be alive, but my foot might not survive. They wanted to amputate. But God had another plan.

A determined doctor fought to save it, and after extensive treatment, my foot was spared. To this day, I still feel the pain. It reminds me of that night, that fall, that moment I wasn't supposed to survive.

The last Near-Death Experience - A Divine Warning

It was a cold, icy night. I had been out drinking with friends, and certain I had a designated driver, until the last moment when they refused to take the wheel. Instead of finding another way home, I made the reckless choice to drive myself.

I was just trying to make it home, but the icy roads had other plans. I lost control. The car spun off an embankment overlooking the highway. At that moment, I should have gone over. I should have crashed onto the road below. But somehow, miraculously, the car stopped just short of the drop.

I sat there, trembling, staring into the darkness beneath me, realizing how close I had come to death. Bystanders rushed to pull me from the vehicle. At the hospital, doctors initially feared my neck was broken. But after repeated imaging, they found nothing, no fracture, no break.

That was when I felt it, God's warning.

He was telling me, *This is your last chance to turn your life around.*

I couldn't ignore the weight of those words echoing in my spirit. As I lay in that hospital bed, surrounded by the beeping of monitors and the soft murmur of nurses in the hallway, I replayed everything in my mind. All the reckless decisions. All the nights I brushed past danger like it couldn't touch me. The people I hurt. The chances I wasted. The calls I didn't return. The love I didn't appreciate.

This wasn't just a brush with death—it was a divine intervention. I didn't just survive a crash that should've killed me. I had been pulled back from the edge of destruction. Literally. Spiritually. Emotionally. God didn't just save my life that night—He spared my soul.

The days after were sobering, not just because I gave up drinking, but because I started facing myself for the first time in a long time. The pain. The guilt. The shame. But also... the hope. Because if God was still speaking to me, then He hadn't given up on me. And if He hadn't given up on me, maybe I shouldn't give up on myself either.

I don't share this for sympathy. I share it because someone needs to hear it. Someone who's one bad decision away from disaster. Someone who thinks they've gone too far. Someone who's been ignoring the signs, just like I was.

That crash wasn't an accident. It was an awakening.

God doesn't always speak through sermons or quiet moments. Sometimes, He shouts through the chaos. Sometimes, He lets the car spin out just to catch it before it falls—to show you how close you've come to losing it all, and how much mercy still surrounds you.

And now? I live differently. I pray more. I listen harder. I value life—not just mine, but the lives of the people around me. I walk with more intention. Because I know, that was my last warning. And I don't take grace for granted anymore.

The Turning Point - A Daughter's Faithful Prayer

My daughters saw what I couldn't. They knew I was running, from my calling, from my healing, from my transformation.

One of my daughters, an apostle, reached out to a minister friend to come and pray over me. They laid hands on me, interceding for my life, declaring healing, purpose, and a new beginning.

And for the first time in a long time, I felt something shift in my spirit. I knew I had been given too many second chances to keep walking the same road. It was time to surrender.

That night, I made a decision. No more drinking. No more reckless choices. No more running from the purpose God had for me. I surrendered completely, throwing myself into my faith, fully, wholeheartedly, without hesitation.

I began attending Bible studies and deliverance classes, seeking mentors who could guide me in my spiritual walk. I surrounded myself with people who didn't just speak about God but truly lived in His presence.

Through prayer, fasting, and deep study of the Word, I began to heal from the inside out. I started to see myself clearly, not as a lost cause, not just as a survivor, but as someone chosen. Everything I had endured—the pain, the trauma, the near-death experiences, was never meant to break me. It was meant to prepare me.

Walking in Purpose

As I stepped into this new season, I discovered my true calling, counseling and mentorship.

I began working with young people, especially young girls who had endured what I had survived. I knew the weight of feeling lost, abandoned, and unworthy. I understood how pain could lead to wrong choices. So, I became an advocate, for women, for healing, for deliverance.

And through this journey, I witnessed the power of transformation, not just in myself, but in those I was helping. God took what the enemy meant for evil and turned it into something powerful. He brought me through the fire without letting it consume me.

A New Beginning

Now, when I tell my story, I don't speak from a place of pain, I speak from a place of victory. Yes, I should have died. Yes, I walked through hell. Yes, I made mistakes.

But God had a plan greater than my past. And He has one for you, too. If you're reading this and feeling lost, know this, your story isn't over. Your trials are not your final destination.

God is waiting for you to surrender, to let Him take the broken pieces and make them whole again. And if He did it for me, a woman drowning in grief, trauma, and near-death experiences.

He can do it for you, too.

Because God never gives up on His children. And He won't give up on you.

CHAPTER 7

Finding Deliverance -
My Journey to True Freedom

For years, I walked through life feeling like I was running out of chances.

I had endured so much pain, heartbreak, struggles, and cycles of bad decisions, yet somehow, God watched over me through it all. He protected me in moments when I should have been lost, broken beyond repair, or even dead. Looking back, I now see just how many times His hand covered me, even when I failed to acknowledge Him.

But at some point, I had to ask myself: How many more chances do I have? Am I on my last one? That question became the turning point in my life.

I had been in and out of church for as long as I could remember, hearing sermons and scriptures, yet I had never truly experienced God, until I made the decision to seek deliverance.

This time, it wasn't just about going to church. It was about surrendering. It was about discovering who God really was, beyond the surface-level understanding I had carried for so long.

The Power of True Deliverance

I started attending Christian classes, and for the first time, I truly grasped the depth of God's word. The Bible was no longer just a collection of stories or verses I had heard in passing, it became a mirror, reflecting my struggles, my wounds, and the healing God was offering me.

I learned about:

- **Deliverance**—the process of breaking free from strongholds
- **Spirits that keep people bound**—fear, rejection, anger, and generational curses
- **The Fruits of the Spirit**—learning to walk in love, patience, and faith
- **True repentance**—not just saying, "I'm sorry," but allowing my heart to change

I had held onto pain, bitterness, regret, and shame for so long that I didn't know who I was without it. But God did.

The Hardest Part: Forgiveness

Forgiveness was one of the hardest parts of my journey. I had to forgive those who hurt me. I had to forgive those who abandoned me. I had to forgive the ones who weren't there when I needed them most.

But more than anything, I had to forgive myself. And that was the hardest part, accepting that God's grace was enough to cover my past. He wasn't holding my mistakes over my head the way the world does. He was simply waiting for me to trust Him completely.

Faith Like a Mustard Seed

There were moments when I felt too weak, too broken, too unworthy. But I always remembered my mother and grandmother speaking about faith as small as a mustard seed.

I never fully grasped the depth of that verse until one day, in one of my women's groups, I was given a tiny bottle filled with mustard seeds.

As I held it in my hands, staring at how small they were, a realization washed over me, God wasn't asking for much. All I needed was faith the size of that tiny seed. If I had that, He would handle the rest.

Breaking Free

I used to think I was *living my best life* when I was out in the world, doing whatever I wanted.

But the truth is, I didn't start living my best life until I surrendered, until I truly understood what it meant to lean on Jesus in every situation, to trust Him completely, and to release the weight I had carried for so long.

Deliverance wasn't a single moment, it was a journey.

A journey of healing. A journey of learning. A journey of unlearning. A journey of growing in faith.

And it was on that journey that I finally understood what it meant to be free, not just free from addictions, struggles, or past mistakes, but truly free in Christ.

A Life Transformed

God had been waiting for me all along. And when I finally reached for Him with everything I had, He met me there. He took my broken pieces and turned them into something beautiful.

I had spent so many years searching—chasing people, validation, status, and temporary fixes to fill a void that only He could satisfy. I thought I could figure it all out on my own, thought I was strong enough to carry the weight of my past, the shame, the guilt, the regrets. But I was drowning, silently, behind a smile that never reached my soul.

There were nights I cried myself to sleep, wondering if I'd ever feel whole again. Days I walked through numb, disconnected, and weary. I kept showing up for everyone else, all while slowly fading inside. But even then—when I felt furthest from grace—God never left me. He was there in every tear, in every silence, in every moment I felt unseen.

And then came the breaking point—the moment when I had nothing left to give and nowhere else to turn. That's when I finally lifted my hands, my heart, and all the wreckage of my life to Him. I stopped pretending. I stopped running. I said, "God, if You're still there... if You still want me... I'm yours."

And He was. He always had been.

He took my broken pieces and turned them into something beautiful. He didn't just patch up the cracks—He created something new. A new mind. A new spirit. A new purpose. He used my pain to birth power, and my story to breathe life into others. What once brought me shame now stands as a testimony of His grace.

Today, I live in the light of that transformation. I still face struggles, but I no longer face them alone. I walk with confidence, not in who I am, but in who He is in me. The love I once searched for in all the wrong places—I found it in Him.

So, when I say my life is transformed, I mean it in every sense of the word. I am not who I was. And thank God... I never have to be again.

CHAPTER 8

Meeting My Husband - A Beacon of Hope and Stability

Life has a way of placing people in our path at just the right time. When I met my husband, I had already endured my share of struggles, heartbreaks, and hard-earned lessons. This was my third marriage, and I entered it with the mindset that life was about me. If things didn't go my way, I was ready to walk away. I didn't truly understand what marriage required, commitment, compromise, and selflessness. Instead of fighting for love, I issued warnings, not realizing that true partnership meant working through the tough times rather than running from them.

We met through a mutual friend, and from the beginning, he was different. He never tried to change me, yet he always encouraged me to be the best version of myself. He became my biggest cheerleader, pushing me to reach for more, whether in my education, career, or faith. No matter what I pursued, he was always there, reminding me that I was capable of achieving whatever I set my mind to.

My husband grew up in a rural area of upstate New York and joined the military at 17. His life experiences shaped him into a man of discipline, responsibility, and deep loyalty. After the military, he became a contractor, traveling to different countries for work, often joking about the "funny money" he made. He was a provider in every sense, not just financially, but emotionally and spiritually. Through every trial and triumph, he stood by me.

When we married, I was living in Oklahoma City, never having been far from my family. My mother and sisters had moved to North Carolina, and though my brother was still in Oklahoma City, my children and grandchildren were in Tulsa. I often felt alone. My husband's job required frequent travel, and during the winter months, I would go to Charlotte. I wasn't used to being away from my mother, so I traveled often. At the same time, I was in and out of the hospital dealing with my foot while trying to complete the required hours for my counseling certification. Despite the challenges, God made a way, allowing me the flexibility to take time off work when I needed it.

One of the greatest blessings during this time was my niece. I had cared for her since she was two, and she kept me grounded, filling my life with purpose even when my husband was away. She was my little companion, traveling with me, keeping me busy, and reminding me that love isn't just about romantic relationships, it's about the people God places in our lives to make a difference. She later graduated, became a mother, and planned a future in the military. Watching her grow reinforced my belief that God assigns us responsibilities not as burdens, but as blessings. Without them, we could easily become reckless, losing sight of what truly matters.

Fourteen years later, here we are, stronger than ever, blessed with sixteen grandbabies, and living proof of God's grace. My husband continues to be my rock, my provider, my encourager, and my best friend. I thank God every day for him, for the lessons we've learned together, and for the unwavering support he has given me.

Looking back, I see now that marriage isn't just about love, it's about growth. It's about choosing each other every day, through every season, and building something that withstands the storms. I had to learn how to be a wife, how to fight for what truly mattered, and how to appreciate the man God placed in my life. And for that, I am forever grateful.

CHAPTER 9

The Motorcycle Mission

Riding a motorcycle had always been a part of my husband's life—his escape, his passion, his freedom on the open road. For me, however, the journey into the motorcycle world unfolded differently.

With my foot injury limiting my ability to shift gears on a traditional bike, my husband made sure I could still experience the thrill of the ride. He bought me a Can-Am Spyder, a three-wheeled Harley-Davidson motorcycle.

That bike was more than just a mode of transportation; it became a symbol of new beginnings, independence, and carving my own path in a world I never expected to be part of.

A Club with a Purpose

Through riding, I met an incredible group of women in Oklahoma City who were part of a motorcycle club. But this wasn't just about riding, it was about purpose. These women were dedicated to giving back, making a difference, and uplifting those in need. That resonated deeply with me, and I knew I had found my place.

Joining the club wasn't just about the road trips and camaraderie, it was about service. We took on projects that directly impacted the community, focusing on education, mentorship, and support.

One of our most rewarding initiatives was helping young girls in high school prepare for college. We provided mentorship, guidance, and resources to help them take the next step in their education, ensuring they had the tools and confidence to succeed.

Another initiative we spearheaded was supporting local teachers. Too often, teachers spend their own money to provide for their students, so we created a program where they could apply for funding to get what they needed, whether it was classroom supplies, activity rugs, snacks, or anything else to enhance their students' learning experience.

Seeing the joy and relief on those teachers' faces when they received help made it all worthwhile.

Finding My Calling on the Road

I have always been passionate about working with youth. From counseling to mentorship, guiding young people, especially within the church, has been at the core of my heart's mission.

Through the motorcycle club, I was able to combine that passion with my love for the open road. Riding allowed me to connect with people from all walks of life, travel to different states, and build lifelong friendships. Every ride had a purpose, and every destination brought new opportunities to inspire, uplift, and plant seeds of hope.

To me, counseling isn't just a profession, it's a calling. Many young people feel lost, unheard, or unsupported. They don't always have positive role models at home, and they may not have anyone telling them they are capable of greatness.

I wanted to be that voice. Through my counseling and involvement in the motorcycle community, I made sure young people knew they had someone in their corner, someone rooting for them. A Mission Bigger Than Myself. I believe God places us in certain positions to fulfill His work. Riding, counseling, mentoring, it all connected back to my mission of guiding and uplifting others.

Eventually, I stepped away from the bike clubs. It became overwhelming to be out on the road on Sunday mornings when I longed to give my all to God. In my weakness, I leaned on Him. I needed Him the most.

Now, I ride solo. When time allows, I enjoy riding with friends, meeting new people, and building healthy relationships.

No matter where life takes me, one thing remains the same: God is the answer, and with Him, anything is possible.

CHAPTER 10

The Fight Against Triple-Negative Breast Cancer

Turning 50 in 2019 was supposed to be a milestone of celebration. Instead, it marked the beginning of one of the toughest battles of my life.

At the time, my husband was in Kuwait, and I had been dealing with a persistent, itchy little knot on my shoulder blade. It was smaller than a dime, yet it constantly irritated me. One day, while chatting with a friend and her nurse friend, they urged me to get it checked out.

But I had other plans. My friends and I were gearing up for a motorcycle trip to Memphis in May, and I wasn't about to let a tiny knot derail my adventure. So, I brushed off their concern, promising myself I'd deal with it when I got back. And that's exactly what I did.

That trip was unforgettable, the open road, the thrill, the laughter. I had no idea my world was about to shift in ways I could never have imagined.

The Diagnosis

After returning home, I went to the military base hospital to have the lump examined. My doctor felt around the area and initially suspected it might be a muscle knot, possibly from a past car accident and the seatbelt impact. But as she continued her examination, she found something else.

She sent me for a biopsy. At the time, I wasn't overly concerned. I even joked with my youngest daughter about it, casually mentioning that I had felt something, but I didn't take it seriously. That all changed the day I got the call.

My mother was visiting from Charlotte and was over at my middle daughter's house. I waited anxiously for the phone call, hopeful yet uneasy. When the expected time passed, I decided I would just go down to the doctor's office myself. But just as I was about to walk out, the phone rang.

I answered. My daughter looked at me. I looked at her. Then, the voice on the other end confirmed what I wasn't ready to hear: Triple-negative breast cancer. I barely processed anything else the woman said. My daughter took the phone and spoke to her while I sat frozen in shock. It felt like the air had been sucked out of the room.

I had always feared breast cancer because my grandmother had it. I had spent years praying my mother would never get it. But in the end, it was me.

The Fight Begins

Triple-negative breast cancer is aggressive. Within weeks, my tumor grew from just a few centimeters to five or six, forcing an urgent shift in my treatment plan. Initially, doctors believed chemotherapy alone might be enough, but as the cancer spread rapidly, radiation became necessary as well.

One of the hardest parts of my treatment was enduring the chemotherapy drug they prescribed, The Red Devil. It had been discontinued for many patients due to its severe side effects, but after consulting with multiple doctors, they agreed it was the best option for my case. So, I braced myself for the battle ahead.

My husband arranged for me to have an apartment in Tulsa so I could be close to my daughters and the cancer center. Though he was still deployed in Kuwait, he made sure I never had to worry about finances. My mom moved back from Charlotte to stay with me throughout my treatments. My daughters, my son, my grandbabies, and my closest friends and family rallied around me, showing up in ways I will never forget. But some people didn't.

I lost a few friends during that time. Some had said, "Call me if you need anything. I'll take you to chemo or radiation." But I never wanted to be a burden. My appointments were early, sometimes as early as 7:30 AM and I didn't feel right asking people to miss work. Instead, I went with family and loved ones who didn't have work conflicts. That decision unintentionally created distance with some friends who felt left out, not realizing I was only trying to spare them. Losing those relationships hurt, but I chose to focus on the ones who showed up without being asked.

The Toll-Physically and Emotionally

Chemotherapy drained me. The Red Devil stripped away my strength, my energy, and, at times, my hope. I already had neuropathy in my foot before I got cancer, but chemo made it worse. Walking became a struggle. My body was weak, and the sickness felt relentless.

Despite my determination, I had to adjust my treatment plan. I cut back on some chemo sessions, and toward the end of radiation, I had to stop early—my body simply couldn't take it anymore. The exhaustion was unbearable. Then came the surgery.

I had a double mastectomy. At first, they attempted reconstruction with implants, but after two failed attempts, my husband and I made the difficult decision to stop trying. That choice was harder than I expected. Losing my breasts wasn't just a physical change, it was an emotional wound. But in the end, my health and survival mattered more.

Still, I grieved. Quietly, painfully. I grieved the body I once had, the dreams I held for how I thought this journey would go, and the illusion of control I'd clung to. I had to rediscover my beauty, my worth, and my strength in new ways. I had to learn to see myself through a different lens—not as someone who lost, but as someone who survived.

A Fighter's Spirit

Through it all, I never thought about dying. Some people, upon hearing my diagnosis, would immediately say, *"You're not going to die."* And I would respond, *"Dying never even crossed my mind."*

I am a fighter. I've always been a fighter. I have 16 grandbabies (at the time, 12), and giving up wasn't an option.

My mother stayed by my side until I rang the bell, signifying the end of my treatment. Then, she moved back to Charlotte. That moment—ringing that bell—was one of the most powerful moments of my life.

One of the most beautiful moments of my journey was when my husband asked me what I wanted as a gift for finishing treatment.

I told him, *"I want to try a Harley."*

And just like that, while still in Kuwait, he arranged for a brand-new Harley-Davidson to be delivered straight from the showroom, fully paid for. It was his way of celebrating my victory, and it meant the world to me.

But more than the gift, this battle revealed my true calling.

A Mission to Serve

During my chemo and radiation treatments, I saw people who had no one. I watched cancer patients sitting alone, waiting for rides that never came, struggling with everyday responsibilities while fighting for their lives.

It broke my heart. I told my husband, *"Once God heals me, I want to start a nonprofit to help people going through cancer who don't have support."* And that's how Pink Sister Inc. was born.

With my husband's help, we launched a foundation dedicated to providing free services to cancer patients, food boxes, transportation to treatments, house cleaning, grocery shopping, financial assistance for gas and essentials, emotional support, and anything else they needed.

Whether they were men, women, or children, we were there for them. I never wanted anyone to feel alone in their fight. I had the privilege of loving and supporting so many, some still fighting, others who have passed on but will always remain in my heart.

More Battles, More Purpose

Just as I was emerging from my own battle, another one struck close to home, my brother was diagnosed with cancer. Though he has beaten it, the effects still linger in his daily life.

Cancer changes you physically, emotionally, and spiritually. But it also teaches resilience. Now, as I continue my work with Pink Sister Inc., I feel a new calling pulling me, to help at-risk youth.

Cancer taught me that life is precious, and it ignited a passion within me to give back in ways I never imagined.

Walking Forward with Purpose

My journey didn't end with my healing; it was only the beginning of something greater. God saw me through the storm, and now, I walk forward with purpose, knowing my pain was never in vain. I survived for a reason, to serve, uplift, and be a light for those still fighting.

CHAPTER 11

Losing My Best Friend - Accidents and Trauma

After battling cancer, I was finally beginning to feel like myself again. The chemo and radiation had taken a toll on my mind, I was forgetful, my thoughts felt scattered, and at times, it seemed as if pieces of me were missing. But glory be to God, my memory was returning, and with each passing day, my mind felt clearer. Just as I was reclaiming my strength, life dealt me another devastating blow.

I lost my best friend to an overdose. She wasn't just a friend, she was family. We had been through everything together. Through the highs and lows, we never argued, never fell out. Our kids grew up side by side, and we even shared a grandson. She knew my heart, and I knew hers. Losing her wasn't just a loss, it was like having a piece of myself ripped away.

To this day, I can't say her name without my eyes welling up or my heart breaking all over again. It still doesn't feel real. The grief is heavy, and some days, I don't know how I carry it. But I know I'm not carrying it alone, God is with me.

She had just told me she was moving back to Oklahoma. I was so excited to have her close again, to pick up where we left off like we always did. But then came that phone call. That morning. Her son, so broken, telling me his mother was gone.

I will never be the same. It changed everything. It broke me in a way I wasn't prepared for. The kind of pain that sucks the air out of the room, that makes your heart shatter in slow motion.

I know she wouldn't want me to sit in sadness. She would want me to keep living, to keep laughing, to keep loving. But grief doesn't come with an instruction manual, it just crashes in, wave after wave. And all you can do is hold on to whatever keeps you afloat. For me, that has been God, my family, and prayer.

The Toll of Trauma

Loss wasn't the only battle I faced. My body had fought its own war, accidents, injuries, surgeries, and scars that serve as reminders of everything I've survived. Every time I sit, stand, or walk, I feel the lingering echoes of my past. My body aches with the weight of trauma, and my mind carries the scars of battles long fought.

Cancer, surgeries, losing loved ones, life-altering injuries, it all stays with me. Some wounds heal, but some pain lingers like a shadow. There are days when I forget things I just said, when my body refuses to move the way I want it to, when the past catches up to me and tries to pull me back.

But I refuse to let it. God didn't bring me this far to leave me.

Through every accident, every loss, and every heartbreak, He has kept me. He has strengthened me. In my weakest moments, when I didn't even have the strength to pray for myself, my children prayed for me. My family prayed for me. And God showed up, like He always does.

Finding Strength in God

Even in my lowest moments, I see His hand at work in my life. I see Him healing me, body, mind, spirit, and soul. Every trial I've faced has led me to deeper faith, a greater purpose, and a stronger testimony.

I am still standing. I am still here.

And as long as I have breath in my body, I will continue to give God the glory, for every mountain I've climbed, every storm I've weathered, and every wound He has healed.

I thank God for my children, my grandchildren, my husband, my family, and my friends, those who lifted me up when I couldn't lift myself. I thank Him for the strength He gives me daily, for the resilience He instilled in me, and for the purpose He continues to reveal.

And though I still grieve, though I still feel the pain, I know God is not done with me yet. He is still writing my story. And through it all, I will keep trusting, keep believing, and keep holding on. Thank You, Lord.

CHAPTER 12

Walking in Purpose

As I embraced my newfound faith, I realized that my pain had prepared me for a greater purpose. I began working with youth who had faced struggles similar to mine, guiding them toward healing and hope. Teaching became more than just a job, it became my ministry.

With every student I taught and every conversation I had, I saw reflections of my younger self, searching, hurting, longing for direction. In those moments, I knew God had placed me here for a reason. My life, once defined by storms, had become a beacon of hope for others navigating their own darkness.

Discovering My Calling

I never set out to be a teacher, a mentor, or a counselor. In fact, there were many times I felt unqualified, like I carried too much baggage, too many scars to lead others. But that's the beauty of God's plan. He doesn't call the qualified; He qualifies the called.

Through my own struggles, I gained something no degree or certification could teach: the ability to connect with those who felt lost, abandoned, or unseen. I understood their pain because I had lived it. That gave me a unique way of reaching them, showing them, they weren't alone and reminding them that their past did not have to define their future.

I dropped out of school in the 9th grade, overwhelmed by life and weighed down by circumstances most young people shouldn't have to face. For a long time, I thought that door was permanently closed. But something inside me kept whispering, "There's more." So, years later, as a mother and full-time employee, I made the bold decision to go back. It wasn't easy. I worked full time, studied late into the night, and poured everything I had into finishing what I had once given up on.

Going back to college and earning my bachelor's degree—and eventually my master's degree—was one of the biggest accomplishments of my life. I carried books in one hand and burdens in the other. All while navigating one of the most difficult seasons of my life: my ex-husband had become a quadriplegic after a tree accident. Though we were no longer together, I remained by his side, helping care for him and making sure our children knew love, strength, and compassion in action.

That time in our lives was hard, but it was also holy. My current husband stood by me, never wavering, never questioning my decision to support my ex in that way. His understanding and heart gave me the space to do what I felt was right for my family. That meant the world to me—and to our children. Being there, watching their father's body slowly shut down, was one of the hardest things we ever walked through. But we walked it together.

As I began working with at-risk youth, I saw firsthand how much they needed someone to believe in them. Many had been written off by the world, labeled as troubled, difficult, or lost causes.

But I knew better. I knew all they needed was someone to see them, love them, and speak life into them.

Now, when I talk to teens and single mothers, I share my story—not to impress them, but to show them what's possible. I tell them about going back to school. About staying the course even when life gets messy. About the power of determination, faith, and community. I remind them that where you start isn't where you have to finish.

Because if God could use someone like me—with a broken past, a dropout record, a heavy heart, and a full plate—He can use anyone.

Becoming an Educator

When I stepped into the classroom, I quickly realized that teaching was about so much more than academics. My students, many of whom had severe and profound needs, weren't just struggling with reading and math. They were struggling with life.

They carried burdens far too heavy for children their age. Some had been abandoned. Others had endured trauma. Many were battling against a system that seemed designed to overlook them.

They reminded me of myself at their age, full of potential but in need of guidance, love, and a safe space to grow. I made it my mission to be that safe space for them.

I knew that if I could reach them emotionally and spiritually, the academics would follow. So, I poured into them, not just with lessons, but with encouragement, patience, and unwavering belief in their ability to rise above their circumstances.

I dedicated extra time to reading and math, knowing that literacy and numeracy were the keys to unlocking opportunities for them. I celebrated their small victories and reminded them that their worth was not defined by a test score.

More than anything, I wanted them to know that someone cared. That they mattered. That their future was not yet written, and they had the power to shape it.

Serving Beyond the Classroom

Beyond teaching, I sought new ways to serve. I became involved in my church's outreach programs, supporting women and youth in need. I began speaking at events, sharing my story, and offering words of hope and encouragement.

Every step I took toward helping others felt like a step closer to fulfilling my divine assignment. One of the most rewarding aspects of my journey has been working with young girls who remind me of myself at their age.

Many of them have faced rejection, low self-esteem, and struggles with their identity. I take them under my wing, guiding them toward confidence and self-worth, reminding them that they are fearfully and wonderfully made.

I also felt called to support other teachers. those who, like me, were navigating the challenges of working with students who needed extra love and attention. I began mentoring new educators, helping them find ways to connect with their students beyond the curriculum.

I knew from my own experience that a single teacher, a single mentor, could change a child's entire trajectory. I wanted to be that person for as many young people as possible.

Finding Peace in My Purpose

Looking back, I see that every storm, every trial, and every painful chapter of my life was leading me to this moment. The girl who once felt lost and broken is now standing in her purpose, using her story to light the way for others.

My journey is far from over. There are still challenges to face, lessons to learn, and lives to touch. But one thing I know for certain, I am exactly where I am meant to be.

Teaching, mentoring, serving, it's not just what I do. It's who I am. And every day, I thank God for leading me here.

Serving Beyond the Classroom

Beyond teaching, I discovered new ways to serve. I became involved in my church's outreach programs, supporting women and youth in need. I began speaking at events, sharing my story, and offering words of hope and encouragement. Every step I took toward helping others felt like a step closer to fulfilling my divine assignment.

One of the most rewarding aspects of my journey has been working with young girls who remind me of myself at their age, girls who have faced rejection, struggled with low self-esteem, and battled with their identity. I take them under my wing, guiding them toward confidence and self-worth, reminding them that *they are fearfully and wonderfully made.*

I also felt called to support fellow teachers those, like me, navigating the challenges of working with students who needed extra love and attention. I began mentoring new educators, helping them find ways to connect with their students beyond the curriculum.

I knew from my own experience that a single teacher, a single mentor, could change a child's entire trajectory. I wanted to be that person, for as many young people as possible.

CHAPTER 13

Transformation, Faith, Sobriety, and Finding My Purpose

When I found out I had cancer, my life changed overnight. The moment I heard the words triple-negative breast cancer, I knew I had to fight with everything in me. And to do that, something had to change.

For years, I had relied on drinking, it was my way of unwinding, coping, and surviving the hard times. But when I received my diagnosis, something deep in my spirit whispered: This stops now.

I didn't need a slow process or a gradual cutting back, I needed to walk away. Cold turkey.

The Decision to Quit-No Looking Back

People often ask me, "How did you stop drinking just like that?"

The answer is simple: God and the family I love so deeply.

I knew that if I was going to beat cancer, I couldn't keep poisoning my body. I had already endured so much, physically, mentally, and emotionally, why add to the battle?

God gave me the strength to walk away, and I never looked back. It wasn't easy. Drinking had been a part of my life, my routine, my social moments. But when faced with the reality of life or death, the choice became clear.

Cancer made me realize that I wanted to live, not just survive, but truly live, fully, intentionally, and with purpose. And to do that, I had to surrender.

I had to release everything that no longer served me, the habits, the fears, the doubts that held me back. If I truly believed in the power of faith and healing, I had to walk in that belief.

My faith gave me courage. My family gave me support.

And my inner strength, the same strength that had carried me through countless battles, pushed me forward. Through this transformation, I leaned on prayer like never before. I began to see things more clearly, feel stronger, and realize that my journey wasn't just about me, it was about what God was preparing me for.

Answering the Call to Ministry

As I grew in my faith, I felt God calling me to something greater.

I had always believed in helping others, but now, I felt a deeper responsibility, a call to ministry. At first, I resisted. I questioned myself, wondering if I was truly qualified.

Who am I to be in ministry? What do I have to offer?

But God doesn't call the qualified, He qualifies the called.

Then, I realized that every experience in my life, every trial, every hardship, every victory, wasn't just for me. It was my testimony. My ministry. My purpose.

So, I stepped into it. I began ministering to others, sharing my story, and encouraging those fighting their own battles. Whether through counseling, speaking, or simply being present for someone in need, I started to understand, this was what I was meant to do.

Finding Fulfillment in Helping Others

There is no greater feeling than realizing your pain had a purpose. Everything I endured, the cancer, the loss, the struggles, was preparing me to be a vessel of hope for others. Through faith, sobriety, and ministry, I have discovered my true calling.

I have witnessed firsthand how God can take brokenness and transform it into something beautiful. I have felt the power of transformation, not just in my own life, but in the lives of those I have been blessed to touch.

Every milestone, every challenge, every victory, it all led me here. And I know this is only the beginning. As I continue on this path, I trust that God will use me in even greater ways. My story is still unfolding, and as long as I have breath in my body, I will keep serving, uplifting, and sharing His love with everyone I meet.

Because this is my purpose.

CHAPTER 14

Friends-The Ones Who Stayed, The Ones Who Left

As I continue on this path, I trust that God will use me in even greater ways. My story is still unfolding, and as long as I have breath in my body, I will keep serving, uplifting, and sharing His love with everyone I meet.

When I Stopped Drinking, the Circle Changed

When I made the decision to quit drinking cold turkey after my cancer diagnosis, I knew it would change me, but I didn't realize how much it would change the people around me.

Before, my life was filled with social moments, clubbing, drinking, partying, things that once felt normal. But when I chose to let that part of my life go, I quickly realized that not everyone was ready to grow with me.

Some friends drifted away. Others avoided me because I was no longer engaging in the things that had once bonded us. And some even questioned my transformation, as if my growth was a personal attack on them.

It wasn't. I didn't stop drinking or partying to judge anyone. I stopped because I wanted to live, truly live, and walk in the purpose God had for me.

But not everyone understood that. Some friends saw my change as a betrayal, as if I had abandoned them. But the truth is, growth isn't about leaving people behind, it's about moving forward in the direction God is calling you. And while I wanted them to come with me, I couldn't force them to change before they were ready.

Friends Who Stayed

Though I lost some friendships, God blessed me with people who stood by my side through it all.

These were the ones who didn't need me to drink or party to love me. They embraced my transformation, celebrated my growth, and prayed for me when I was too weak to pray for myself.

They didn't just tolerate my journey, they encouraged it. They reminded me of who I was becoming, not who I used to be. And those are the friendships worth holding.

Friendships During Ministry

When I stepped into ministry, my friendships shifted even more. Not everyone was comfortable with my new role. Some supported me from a distance, while others disappeared completely.

I learned that not everyone will celebrate your calling. Not everyone will understand why you choose to walk with God instead of following the world. But that's okay. True friendship isn't about convenience, it's about loyalty, love, and understanding. Those who truly love you will support your journey, even when it looks different from theirs.

Lessons in Loyalty and Love
Losing friends hurt, but it also made me stronger. It taught me that:

- Not everyone is meant to stay in your life forever. Some people are only meant for a season, and when their time is up, you must let them go in peace.

- Friendship isn't about quantity, it's about quality. I'd rather have a few real friends than a crowd that only loves me when I fit their expectations.

- True friends love you for who you are, not for what you do. They don't need you to drink with them, party with them, or mirror their lifestyle. They love you simply for who you are at your core.

- God never takes without giving. Every time I lost a friend, He placed the right people in my life, ones who filled the space with love, encouragement, and faith.

Moving Forward with Love
Now, instead of chasing friendships that were never meant for me, I invest in relationships rooted in love, faith, and mutual respect.

I surround myself with people who lift me up, pray for me, and walk this journey of life with me, no matter where it leads. And even for those who left, I hold no bitterness.

I still love them, still pray for them, and still hope that one day they see what I see, that life with God is greater than anything the world can offer.

Friendship has shaped me, strengthened me, and taught me that those meant to be in my life will always remain. And for that, I am truly grateful.

CHAPTER 15

Family, Faith, and the Ties That Bind

F amily is the foundation of who we are, the place where we learn, grow, and become the people God has called us to be.

Over the years, my relationships with my siblings, parents, children, and grandchildren have evolved in ways I never expected. Some bonds were tested, some grew stronger, and others were completely transformed. But through it all, faith has remained the unbreakable thread that holds us together.

Faith and Family-A Shared Journey

When I fully surrendered my life to God and picked up my cross, something shifted, not just within me, but within my family as well. There is something powerful about serving a God who restores, strengthens, and brings people together in ways we could never have imagined.

Now, my entire immediate family is in church. That is nothing but God's grace.

- My daughter is an apostle, leading others and walking boldly in her calling. Watching her grow spiritually and step into a leadership role in the church fills my heart with gratitude.

- My son is in South Carolina, raising a beautiful family of four boys and instilling in them the values that will guide them through life.

- My daughters, my mother, and my grandchildren are all faithfully serving in the church. They are not just attendees, they are engaged in worship, ministry, and service.

- My brothers and sisters stand by me in every way, showing unwavering love and support.

- My nieces, nephews, and cousins are my extended strength, encouraging me on my journey and reminding me that they are proud of the path I am walking.

Revisiting Relationships with Parents and Siblings

My relationship with my mother has been a journey of love, growth, and understanding. At 73 years old, she remains deeply devoted to her faith, still going to church, still participating, still inspiring. Her unwavering presence in my life has been a guiding force, and now, more than ever, our bond is strengthened through faith.

Over the years, my siblings and I have grown closer. Life has taken us in different directions, but at our core, we have always been family first. Faith has drawn us even nearer, giving us a shared foundation to lean on. We may not always see eye to eye, but one thing is certain, we stand together.

Motherhood, Grandmotherhood, and the Blessing of Legacy

Being a mother has been one of my greatest joys, but becoming a grandmother has given my life even deeper purpose. Watching my grandchildren grow in the church, seeing them participate in worship and ministry, and witnessing them embrace God's love fills me with unspeakable joy.

I used to worry about whether I had done enough for my children, whether I had taught them well, whether they would be okay. But now, as I watch them walk their own paths, raising their children with faith and love, I know in my heart that God has them, just as He has always had me.

More than just blood, family is a sacred bond, a spiritual connection we nurture, protect, and grow.

The Power of God in Family Relationships

Faith didn't just change me, it transformed the way I love, forgive, and show up for my family.

There were times when relationships felt strained, when misunderstandings and distance-built walls between us.

But God is a God of restoration, and He has healed places I once thought were beyond repair.

- Faith has helped me forgive where I once held on to hurt.

- Faith has helped me appreciate my family more deeply.

- Faith has reminded me that love is not just a feeling, it is an action.

Walking in Faith, Together

Now, as I continue growing in my purpose, I hold onto the greatest gift God has given me—a family united in faith. No matter where life takes us or what challenges we face, we are covered, blessed, and walking this journey hand in hand. And for that, I give all glory to God.

There is something sacred about knowing that we don't walk alone. In a world that often tries to pull us apart, our faith binds us together. It's the prayers whispered in the quiet, the scriptures shared during tough times, and the worship that lifts our spirits even in the valley. It's the way we show up for each other—not just in joy, but in struggle. That unity, that spiritual bond, is what keeps us grounded.

Each member of my family brings something unique to our walk: a strength, a gift, a testimony. We laugh together, cry together, and lift each other up in prayer when the burdens feel heavy. We may not always have the answers, but we always know where to turn—into the presence of God, together.

When one of us grows weary, the others become the strength. When one of us celebrates, we all rejoice. Our faith is not just a belief—it's a lifestyle, a shared commitment to honor God in how we live, love, and lead.

And as I continue to step into what God has called me to do, I know that the power of our unity, rooted in Him, will carry us through anything. We are not perfect, but we are covered. We are still growing, but we are guided. We are still becoming, but we are blessed.

And for that, I give all glory to God.

About the Author

Leeann Deon is a survivor, a warrior, and a woman of unwavering faith.

Born into adversity, she has endured the trials of mental and physical abuse, the grief of losing loved ones too soon, and the overwhelming responsibility of becoming a teenage mother after being sexually violated. But through every fire, Leeann found strength in God, refusing to let her past define her future.

From brokenness to breakthrough, her journey is one of resilience, faith, and purpose. As the founder of *Pink Sister Inc.*, Leeann has dedicated her life to helping others heal— whether through advocacy, mentorship, or ministry. Her passion lies in uplifting youth and young adults, supporting those facing trauma, and walking alongside individuals seeking restoration.

Now, in *Faith in the Fire*, Leeann invites readers into the raw and unfiltered truth of her life—a testimony of pain, redemption, and unshakable faith. Through her words, she hopes to inspire others to find healing, embrace their power, and walk boldly in their purpose.

Beyond her work as a Special Education teacher and missionary, Leeann is a devoted wife, a proud mother of four, and a loving grandmother to sixteen. She is the daughter of a strong woman of God, a sister, a friend, and an aunt. She continues to show up for the children of her friends who passed away too soon and is a woman who cherishes the deep bonds of family and faith.

When she is not working, Leeann enjoys being in the wind on her Harley-Davidson motorcycle and spending quality time eating, laughing, and making memories with family and loved ones. With God at the center of all she does and a heart full of gratitude, she is still writing her story—one chapter at a time. She prays this book is a blessing to you on your healing journey.

Acknowledgements

First and foremost, I give all glory and honor to God. Without His grace, I would not be here to share this testimony. Through every trial, He has been my strength, my refuge, and my guide. This book is a testament to His faithfulness, and I pray it touches the lives of those who read it.

To my family and loved ones—thank you for standing by me through the storms. Your love, prayers, and encouragement have been the foundation upon which I've rebuilt my life.

To my children—you are my greatest blessings, and your strength inspires me daily.

To my Pink Sister Inc. family and everyone who has supported this mission, thank you for believing in the vision God placed in my heart. Your unwavering support fuels the work we do, and I am grateful beyond words.

To my mother, Gail Hersey—my first love, my biggest supporter, and the woman who taught me what it means to be strong and resilient. Your love has been my foundation, and your unwavering belief in me has carried me through life's hardest moments. Thank you for always being there, for always showing up, and for instilling in me the strength to keep pushing forward.

To my children, Meleiaa, Tyler, Shayna, and Akeyiaa—I can't thank you enough. You are true blessings in my life, and I am beyond proud to be your mother. The love, joy, and strength you bring to my life keep me going every single day.

To my 16 beautiful grandchildren—you are my MVPs! My life would not be the same without each and every one of you. The joy you bring me is beyond words, and Gramam loves you more than you could ever know.

To my husband, thank you for always believing in me, even when you can't see the vision. Your support, your love, and your willingness to stand by me through every high and low mean more than words can express. You love me through it all, and for that, I am forever grateful.

To everyone who has prayed for me, encouraged me, or simply spoken life into me when I needed it most—thank you. You may never know how much your kindness meant, but I do, and I hold it in my heart.

Lastly, to the woman reading this book who feels lost, broken, or unsure of her future—this is for you. Know that God sees you, He hears you, and He has a plan for your life. Walk in faith, even when the fire burns hottest, because on the other side is the victory He has prepared for you.

With love and gratitude!

Leeann

www.ingramcontent.com/pod-product-compliance
Lightning Source LLC
Chambersburg PA
CBHW051330120626
46547CB00016B/2477